CARFREE LIVING

CARFREE LIVING:

Happy in the Not So Fast Lane

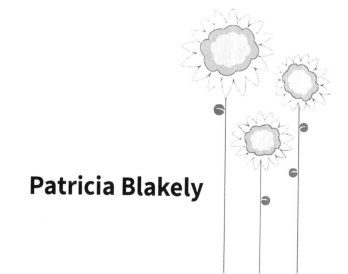

Patricia Blakely

To my sweet surprises,
my grandchildren
Max, Lulu, Cooper and Lena

Table of Contents

Acknowledgments

I'd like to thank friends and family for their support and encouragement in the writing of this book—especially readers of the manuscript in its many iterations, Nordis Heyerdahl, Ginny May, Steve Peters, Kay Marcotte, Dennis Keuper, members of my writing group Sande Turner, Chris Howard, Molly Hill, Jeanie Hansen, my soul friend Jan Dougherty, encourager in all things, and my spiritual director Julie Neraas. I'd like to thank Scott Edelstein, my editor, and Patti Frazee, my designer, for their expert help and advice. This project would still be in manilla file folders if it weren't for them all.

I'd like to thank my ride-share friends and friends who usually came to my house because it was easier for me to host than to find my way to their houses. The list would go on for pages, but you know who you are, and I am deeply grateful to you all.

And most of all, I'd like to thank Mike McLaughlin, dearest friend, whose belief in my carfree project never wavered, though mine sometimes did, and whose quiet, steady encouragement kept it on track in countless ways.

X

A Note to Readers

This little book is for anyone who has thought about going carless, but hasn't taken any concrete action yet.

Maybe you don't know anyone who has done it. That was true for me. Maybe your friends would be a little shocked, as mine were.

Maybe you don't know exactly how to begin and would like to benefit from someone else's experience. Maybe you are almost ready, but just need a little nudge. I hope my story will give you the kickstart you're looking for.

I began my car story in the form of diary entries. I wrote them to give me courage. To help me see my progress. To let me sound off when things weren't going so well. To find a way to smooth out a rough patch and make a better plan. I wrote them to give me some distance from the day-to-day experience and gain perspective, a longer view. Was the experiment working? Did I want to continue?

Going carless was not an instant makeover for me. I soon realized it was a lifestyle change that would take some time adjusting to. At the same time, mine is not a zero impact story. I wasn't looking for an impossibly stringent transportation diet. I wanted something that was sustainable over the long haul. Going carless did not fundamentally change me or my life. I have the same work, the same friends, the same connections to my city and all it has to offer. But it did tweak my life for the better in many ways, which was the big surprise.

Is the carfree life for you? Perhaps my experience will help you decide.

I hope you will find here the information and the inspiration to try it out, to see for yourself. If you do, I promise you will discover the peculiar freedom that comes with letting someone else take the driver's seat. You will experience the exhilaration of saving lots of money (and gas!) while de-accelerating the pace of your life. You will find healthier patterns automatically built into your day. A growing sense of adventure and connection. And a surprising peace—in making smaller circles with greater joy.

I wish you all success and happiness in the not-so-fast lane.

Patricia Blakely
Minneapolis, November 12, 2012

Carless in Minneapolis

My sister Paulette called recently from Pennsylvania to say that her nephew is in a coma because of a near-fatal car accident. He was driving on a winding, hilly, two-lane road in bad winter weather. Now he is in the hospital, lingering between life and death.

My brother Dennis calls this morning from Maryland. His wife Odile was in a bad car accident, too. She blanked out, lost control of the car, and swerved into oncoming traffic. A van coming from the opposite direction turned away to avoid her, but hit her anyway, then rolled over and hit a third car. Her car and the van were totaled. Miraculously, all three drivers were OK. But she is in the hospital for observation.

This afternoon, I had my own accident. I was waiting at a stop light in a line of cars. The light turned green and the line slowly started moving. Then someone ahead of me stopped suddenly. I stopped, too, but, in my rear view mirror I saw the driver behind me with his head down, reaching for something low and continuing to come at me. *Bang!* I mentally scanned my body for actual pain or injury. Nothing. We stopped at the nearest gas station, inspected our cars for damages, and found only a slightly dented license plate on his. We shook hands and got back into our cars, feeling very lucky.

A fortune from a fortune cookie surfaces in a stack of papers to file: *If you drove here, walk home. Repeat: Walk home.* I have never seen a fortune like this one before. But today I'm taking it as a forecast of things to come.

In Minnesota, it's sunny and cold. Minus 3 degrees and minus 22 degrees wind chill. The forecast is for temperatures below zero all day.

At 9:00 I go to Dunn Bros, my neighborhood coffee shop, to warm up and to gather my courage before I try to get in my car again. I'm hoping the freezing rain that clamped my car doors shut will melt a little. Earlier this morning I tried to get in the driver's door, but it wouldn't budge. I tried *all* my doors. None of them would open, although the hatch door in the back seemed ready to give way before the others. The thought of climbing in the back door and crawling over two sets of seats sent me to the coffee shop to think of a better approach.

At 10:00 I try a second time. With one desperate yank, I get the driver's door open. I start the car and drive to a neighborhood mechanic. For the past week, the windshield wiper fluid has refused to flow. I'm hoping he can fix it quickly and cheaply.

But on this bitterly cold Monday morning, his parking lot is jammed and his tiny waiting room is full of stranded motorists with much bigger problems than mine.

"Can you help me?"

"No way. Not till later. Can you call back at 2:00?"

"Sure."

I drive a mile or so to Linden Hills to do a little Christmas shopping. At 11:15 I'm ready to go home, but now my car won't start.

I don't have my cell phone with me, so I go to the nearby bakery to call AAA. I wait patiently at first, knowing I'm not the only one needing rescuing this morning. I feel grateful to be inside the bakery and warm. I read *The Onion* movie reviews, but eventually the bakery's background music gets to me: silent movie train wreck music, cartoon soundtracks, nerve-jangling blue grass.

I start counting the buses that pass by. Then I lose count. It's too depressing. I could have taken a bus to go shopping and been home by now.

At 12:30, the AAA serviceman shows up in a van, but he can't get my battery to work. He disappears in a flash, saying the tow truck will be "coming soon." "Soon" turns out to be a couple of hours later.

I remember half boasting that my 2002 Subaru would be my last car. I was planning to drive it into the ground. With only 58,000 miles on it, I thought that would be years from now. But I'm beginning to see the advantages of being without a car altogether. No windshield scraping, no snow brushing, no AAA towing, no expensive repairs.

At 1:30 I call AAA again on the bakery phone for an update. Now the ETA is 1:50. It turns out they're pretty close. My rescuer shows up at 2:15. But it's been almost three hours since I called the first time. I'm on the verge of frustrated tears. Amazingly, the tow truck driver gets my battery going and my car started. So I drive it back to the mechanic. The day has taken its toll on everyone.

"Just have a seat and we'll get to you as soon as we can," the weary owner says.

In his cramped waiting room there are five people and three metal chairs. A large woman, swathed in a heavy coat, sits lumpily in one of them, in a stupor. Apparently she poured hot water on her frozen car door this morning. That's a total no-no in the Great Northland. It makes everything worse, like licking a frozen metal post. I can see through the glass to the garage area where two men are struggling to loosen the massive ice jam she created.

A middle-aged woman and her frail elderly mother stand near the door. The woman is talking loudly on her cell phone, apparently trying to reach her husband.

"I've got a husband—he's better than AAA," she jokes awkwardly.

He needs to come to the service station with his keys because her car is fixed, but it's in the lane of the mechanic's crowded lot—and it's running—with the keys locked inside it. Her car is blocking the entire lane. She's embarrassed, as is her mother, who apparently forgot her cane on the way out of the service station and had to retrieve it, indirectly causing the current upset. They are—unsuccessfully—trying to make light of the inconvenience they are causing everyone else.

My car is blocked, too, as is the next one to be serviced, but neither can be worked on until the woman gets her husband's keys.

The woman keeps calling home. No one answers. Finally, her teenage son answers and says, "Dad is still in the shower." He tried to get him out of the shower, but, he says, "Dad takes long showers." The woman relays this to us all.

I can't take it any longer. Bitterly cold or not, car or no car, I tell the mechanic, "I'm walking home. Here's my number. Just call me, when you can find out what's wrong, OK? Thanks so much!"

I'm relieved to be walking...for the first half block.

Then, for nine and a half more blocks, I cover my nose and mouth with my scarf, and lean into the icy wind, hunkering down. It is a seriously cold march.

At 4:30, eight hours after I left home, I'm thrilled to be back.

The saga of the disabled car goes on. At 9:00 the next morning I call the garage. They haven't checked to see if my car is starting up yet, but "we will and we'll call you." I cancel my dental appointment—with apologies. I thought I'd have a car by this morning, but I don't. I've done everything I can this morning without the car. But now I need to do some errands. I'm getting antsy.

At 10:15, the mechanic calls. My car started right up after a new battery and a $217 bill. I should have checked the battery in the fall, but I didn't. At least now, I have a road-worthy car. Unfortunately, $217 is going to seriously deplete my Christmas budget.

It's ten degrees above zero and sunny. There is no wind chill. A nice day for a walk back to the service station. Brilliant new-fallen snow bounces the sunlight in a thousand directions.

I pick up my car and do errands that could not easily be done without a car: mailing my Christmas packages, picking up a five-ream box of computer paper, and stocking up on holiday groceries.

People in the grocery store say with a smile, "It's almost balmy today!" And they mean it. I'm from

California originally, so I think *they* are balmy, not the day. Still, it feels thirty degrees warmer today than it did yesterday and we all feel the uptick in our bodies and our spirits.

In the evening, I debate about going dancing downtown. To go anywhere, I need to scrape frost off my windshield. It's a struggle to keep frost from clouding the windshield on the inside as well. The car never warms up completely. The air from my heater is an arctic blast.

A cab would be the perfect solution for a winter night out, but I don't call a cab. I'm feeling poor after paying to get my car fixed, and I can't justify the $12 each way for a cab ride. I don't go dancing.

I need a place to park my car while I'm away for the holidays. It's a challenge. I can't find an empty garage in my urban neighborhood, not even an off-street parking spot. I can't leave it on the street because of snow emergency plowings that could happen while I'm gone. My mechanic suggests checking with a classic car auto body place nearby. I do and I learn that what I want is called "short-term storage." This place charges $600 for the winter or $100 per month. Al, the amiable owner, tells me he has a space available.

I'll be away one week in New York City for

Christmas with my family and then two weeks in Mexico. There will be a week in between when I'm back home, so I decide to go carless that week. I'm not crazy about paying $100 to store my car. With that item, my extra car-related costs this month are up to $317. But I tell Al, OK.

On Sunday, I drive to church. It's still very cold. Ice has frozen on the windshield. Deep snow is in the streets. Home again, I remember to park on the emergency route street for the night. Minneapolis and St. Paul have very strict and complicated rules for parking on the street in the winter. If you do not obey them to the letter, your car will be towed and you will pay dearly to get it back.

I've been thinking for some time about how to use my car less. I've even wondered if I could give it up entirely. If I could get along without it in January, the coldest month in Minnesota, I might have a chance of going carless the rest of the year. This month will be my experiment in carless living.

On an impulse, I decide to ride the bus downtown to my friend Ginny's condo. It's a frigid wait on the corner a half block from my house, and I almost give up, but a northbound #6 bus finally comes. I check my watch. Was the wait only ten minutes? Well, yes, actually, it was.

Inside the bus, it's warm and cozy. Riding on the mezzanine level of this new electric hybrid bus gives me a new perspective on my city. It's like watching the world go by from a parade float. It's my first Minneapolis bus ride in about 30 years. I feel like a little kid on a joy ride.

Monday at 9:00 am, it's 6 below zero. I'm on my way to the airport to spend Christmas with my son Alexander and his family in New York CIty. But first I need to stop at Lunds market to pick up some lefse, flat Norwegian bread that's roughly a cross between a pita and a tortilla, made from potatoes. It's a tradition. It wouldn't be Christmas without a little lefse from the North country.

I load my car with luggage and holiday gifts. My car is frosty, but it starts and I take off toward Lunds just five blocks away. My next stop will be the classic car place where I'll store my car for a month. Then, the airport.

But when I come out of the grocery store, my car won't start!

From the store phone, I call Al at his shop. It's about 10 blocks away. He is very kind. He says he'll send his nephew Spencer over right away with a battery box.

While I wait for Spencer, I call an airport taxi to pick me up at Al's at the last possible time to make my flight. I need all the time I have left to get my car to Al's. My young rescuer shows up. He's a slim blond teen in jeans and a parka. He's friendly enough, but he's a young man of few words. I wonder, is this the first time he's done this? It turns out he knows what he's doing with my car, but he can't make it go. The engine turns over but doesn't fire, he explains. I'm learning more than I want to know about disabled cars in winter. He loads my luggage in the back of his truck and takes me to his uncle's place. I give Al my car keys and $100 for the month's storage.

I call my mechanic. Fortunately today is Monday and he's open. He says he'll tow the car to his place "later in the day." Al offers to take my keys to the mechanic.

I hand $20 tips to Al and his nephew. Spencer's face lights up, which makes my day. A minute later, I see a welcome sight: the airport taxi at the curb, as promised. I just pray the mechanic will find my car in the grocery store parking lot when he goes to tow it.

The prospect of life without a car is beginning to seem positively sane.

New York City is perhaps the best place in America to live happily without a car. Everything is close together and designed for people who walk. And that's what my family does.

My son Xander and my grandson Max meet me at the JFK airport baggage claim. We retrace the route they took to get to the airport. We take the Air Train and the Long Island Railroad train to Penn Station, where we catch the #2 subway to 72nd and Broadway. We walk four blocks to their apartment on 70th and Columbus.

We do our Christmas shopping on foot and by bus. We walk to a nearby Upper West Side coffee shop, to warm up, chat and watch the busy world go by. We cross Central Park on foot to reach another coffee shop on the East Side at 70th and Lexington. It's my daughter-in-law Natasha's favorite.

I walk to Lincoln Center to hear Renee Fleming in her second to last performance of *Thais*. I go with a friend who, like me, is willing to watch an entire opera while standing. There are a few $16 standing-room-only seats available in what they call the Family Gallery—the very last row, just under the ceiling. There are also some $200 seats in front. They are out of the question. But I just spent that much on my car: my mechanic charged me $233 to tow it to his garage and replace the spark plugs.

Over the next few days, we walk to do normal

errands, grocery shop, and get a passport renewed. We walk to the American Museum of Natural History. We walk to Central Park, a block away, every day. There my grandchildren run and bike and play with school mates. It's their glorious front yard, backyard and wilderness. On Christmas Eve, we splurge and take a cab to services at St. Bartholomew's Episcopal Church in Midtown.

On the last day, I taxi to JFK from Manhattan. And I taxi home from the Minneapolis airport. It's after dark when I arrive and it's 12 degrees outside. The taxi is handy and warm inside.

I've been back less than fourteen hours and I need to deal with my car. It's in storage now at Al's, but I need to go to my mechanic to pay the $233 bill. So I walk there in sunny, sub-zero weather. I ask him, "Since when was replacing spark plugs a significant repair job?" He shrugs. "That's not a big bill," he says. Maybe not for him.

I keep comparing repair bills to other things— Christmas gifts, opera tickets, other luxuries. When I compare them to taxi rides, though, taxis look like an amazing deal. Two recent repairs, over $500. The average taxi fare with tip is what? $10 $15 $20? I don't know. But, whatever, $500 is a lot of taxi rides.

Last summer I had a really big car repair bill. $1500. My brakes needed work. At the time bus fares were $1.50. I realized—with a jolt—that $1500 would cover 1000 bus fares! One car repair versus how many *years* of bus riding?

The mechanic tells me, "You're not driving your car enough. That's why you're having spark plug problems."

The next morning, Rick, a coffee shop buddy, agrees with my mechanic. "Not enough commuter miles to burn clean," he says.

For the first time, I seriously consider selling my car. Maybe, I should keep it in storage another month and see what life is like without it.

There's something ironic about taking a bus to a massage therapist. The day is bright and cold. The high today will be no more than 15 degrees. I dress in lined leather boots, heavy wool socks, long silk underwear, a wool turtleneck sweater, a heavy wool cardigan, a down parka with a fur trimmed hood, lined leather mittens, and a warm woolen scarf, wound several times around my neck. This is therapeutic?

I check my bus schedule for route #23 going east. This bus stops a block from my house, but it runs only every half hour. I panic a little because I have just a few minutes to get to the stop in time. But on icy sidewalks, I can't walk fast! I make it to the stop, then realize I don't have the right change. The fare is $1.75. And I have only a five-dollar bill in my wallet. I give it to the bus driver. She can't give me change, but she says, "Oh, you could have asked other passengers for change. Here, take these two extra passes. They're good for two days."

Frankly, today, I would have been happy to pay $5 just to get out of the cold. I sit back and enjoy the ride across town.

I'm close enough to the front of the bus to eavesdrop on a lively conversation between the driver and a woman sitting across from her in the first passenger seat. They are chatting like old friends. I wonder, is there a community of drivers and regular riders? Or do the gregarious riders tend to sit in that first seat? (I eventually learn that the answer to both questions is yes.)

Twenty minutes later, the bus drops me off a block from the massage therapist's studio.

On the ride home, I wonder how many different things I can do while riding a bus: I can't read like some people do because reading in a moving vehicle makes me queasy, but I can make mental grocery lists, think of things to be grateful for, day-dream. It occurs to me that this is a great time to do nothing at all, a rare opportunity to take a real break—to sit, breathe, be.

I'm riding the westbound #23 bus and chatting with another rider. He tells me he's been carless since 1990. I'm impressed and want to know more.

His name is Steve. He's pleasant and articulate. He's 54, a former chef, and is now on disability because of arthritis. But he is an avid bicyclist and bus rider.

"Cycling is easier on my body than walking," he explains.

He tells me he loves the Twin Cities. He's not a native. He moved from California to Iowa City in 1990. He gave up car driving then, and never looked back. Compared to Iowa City, apparently, Minneapolis is " a great commuter town for cyclists." And, he insists, "You can get anywhere by bus."

But his "anywhere" doesn't include the suburbs. "Well, not the suburbs. I've never been to the suburbs and I've been here 10 years," he says.

Then he says, "Most of the year I bike wherever I want to go." I marvel at this, but he shrugs, and says, "My grandmother rode a bike into her 80s. She drove a tractor, too. But never a car."

"It's a mindset," he adds. "And, in the winter, you just have to get the right clothes."

Steve is wearing heavy boots and a storm parka.

He's also sporting a multi-colored wool knit hat, the kind made in Bolivia with earflaps and braided ties. It doesn't detract one bit from his rugged outdoors look. In fact, it enhances it in an Urban Outfitters sort of way. The biking and the walking weren't doing his physique any harm, either. He looks trim and strong. He points to a small back pack. "I can get two days' groceries in this."

Lake Street and Hennepin Avenue. My stop and his. We get off the bus and might have chatted a bit more, but a fellow approaches us to ask, "Any change? I'm out of a job." We each give the man a dollar and, with a friendly wave, go our separate ways.

Sunday, on my bus ride home, I notice an older Asian woman with a short gray bob sitting across the aisle. She is dressed mostly in white, from her sweatshirt and turtleneck to her white sneakers. Is she a nurse? A hospital attendant?

A vivid green coat sprawls around her shoulders. Bright red leather gloves lay at her side, along with a couple of shopping bags.

I see now that one meaning of "public transportation" is that your ride is public, as in "open to or shared by all." What you wear, what you carry, how you interact or don't interact with your driver or your fellow passengers—it's all on display for the rest of us to see.

This woman has a smooth, serene face. Her eyes look around in a relaxed, alert way. Her lips are moving ever so slightly. I think she is about to address me, but then I realize that's not it. She is intent on something else. In one hand, covered slightly by one of her bags, she is holding a rosary of wooden beads. The beads are moving slowly through her fingers.

Another thing you can do while riding a bus: pray.

Today is bright and sunny, and there is no wind, so I almost enjoy waiting for the #23 bus to take me across town for my massage appointment. I don't mind the 15-minute wait to catch a bus on the way home, either.

It's the day after Barack Obama's inauguration and the bus driver is gleeful about it. He's an older man, with neatly trimmed hair, wire-rimmed glasses and a grey wool cardigan. He chats animatedly with the young woman who sits across from him. She's wearing heavy-duty work clothes and looks weary. She says she's happy about it, too. But she works for the city, driving a recycling truck, and her hours have recently been cut. She's worried about her job.

My carless life is expanding my experience of my

city and my country. Riding the bus is a way for me to eavesdrop on the times, on what others are thinking and feeling. In many ways, it's much better than reading the newspaper—more vivid, more direct, more real.

On the way home, I stay on the bus a few blocks past "my" stop and get off in Uptown, in order to pick up some groceries. I enjoy the walk home. Could the temperature be above freezing? I see some melted patches in the streets.

At 7:30 am I take a northbound #6 bus downtown to 8:00 contemplative prayer at St. Mark's Cathedral. The bus is packed with young professionals on their way to work. I get to the Cathedral in plenty of time.

After 30 minutes of group silence, most of my contemplative friends migrate to a nearby coffee shop for 30 minutes of friendly chatter. Then I catch the southbound #6 bus back to Uptown. The rush hour fare is $2.25 and I can use the transfer ticket for 2 1/2 hours, any number of times, going in any direction. So, I come home on the transfer ticket. It feels like a real bargain.

In the afternoon, I take a cab to my clinic in St. Louis Park, the nearest suburb to the west, to see a foot specialist. I could take a bus, but it involves a transfer and I don't know how long the total ride will take and

I'm afraid to miss my appointment. I want to check out my feet. If I'm going to walk more than ever, *every day*, I want to take good care of them. I have bunions on both feet and I don't want to make matters worse. But my doctor says, "If you're walking three miles a day without serious pain, and you can dance in the evening, you're fine."

Marie is sitting in her favorite French restaurant in downtown Minneapolis. I've joined her for lunch to talk about going carless. I met Marie recently at a friend's party. When I heard that she was living happily in Minneapolis without a car, I wanted to know more.

A petite woman, impeccably groomed, Marie may be in her late 70s. It's hard to tell. With clear blue eyes, medium-short blonde hair and vivid red lips, she is beautiful and self-assured.

A couple of years ago, she said, she had come to Minneapolis from Hawaii—where she had lived for six years—and was struck by the changes in the city. She was pleased to be living in a high-rise condo in downtown Minneapolis, but she had some reservations about driving here.

"Compared to what it was, this traffic is terrible. And there's no place to park."

She also noticed her older friends were not driving all that well. "Poorer depth perception. Slower response time." They were having "little mishaps." She found she wasn't comfortable riding in their cars and began wondering if she should stop driving herself.

Many years ago, she'd lived a carfree life in Chicago and thought she could do it again in Minneapolis, but hesitated to make the change. She was older now. "And the winters are a lot tougher here."

Then, Marie had her own fender bender. It was her personal turning point. Her decision was made.

She discovered that she could live very well without a car in Minneapolis. She walks a lot, which she knows is "just plain good for me." She knows she is saving a significant amount of money, even when she takes a cab. "I take buses when it's convenient and cabs when it's not."

"Now I don't worry about fender benders or flat tires. Or traffic or parking. And who needs car payments? I'd rather buy shoes!"

As for getting around the city for daily errands, shopping and socializing, she makes it sound easy. "All it takes is a little planning and a little originality," she insists. "And small adjustments, like in your wardrobe. In weather like this I really bundle up."

But Marie does her bundling in her own stylish way. No bulky down parka and storm boots for her. On this brilliant but chilly afternoon, she's in a zippered black mink jacket, dark wool pencil skirt, opaque black hose and—why am I not surprised?—beautiful high-heeled black leather boots.

As we leave the restaurant, Marie pulls out her sunglasses, and says with a smile as bright as the day, "I love the outside air, don't you?"

Then she sets out briskly toward her condo seven blocks away.

I'm definitely ready to try one more month without my car. I call Al, the guy who is storing it. He says he can keep my car another month, for another $100. So, I agree to leave it there. He also says, in passing, that he likes my car and would buy it from me if I ever decided to sell it.

I also call my car insurance company. I want to know if I can get a reduction on my insurance payment for the months that I store my car. They say, "No, only if you have two cars and you store one of them."

My friend Nordis calls. "Do I want to go with her to an art exhibit at the University tonight?"

"No, thanks," I say. "It's just too cold."

If I had my car, I might have gone with her and then gone dancing afterwards, because Friday is my favorite night for Argentine tango. But without a car, I stay home. I bake peanut butter cookies instead and I read a book. And I wonder, is this carless life limiting my horizons? Or is it opening them up? Is it contributing to a more active life? Or a more contemplative one?

Walking is getting built into my day, almost every day, by necessity. That's a good thing. It's keeping me mentally on my toes as well, requiring me to create new solutions, solving daily logistics problems like some people solve a daily sudoku puzzle.

Today, for example. It's below zero. Bright and sunny, but bitterly cold. I need groceries, but it's much too cold to walk 10 blocks to and from the nearest market.

My new severe weather shopping strategy is to wait till midday, likely the warmest part of the day, take the northbound #6 bus to Uptown on a non-peak fare of $1.75, do my errands and go back home on a southbound #6 bus. On the same fare. It can be done in an hour.

I don't mind adjusting to the weather or paring down on the number of things I try to accomplish in a day. But I do mind debating with friends about places to go, when both of us know that, for many destinations, I'm dependent on them for transportation. That is the puzzle I need to work on now. I want to find a way to make this more equitable, more reciprocal.

This carless experiment is having unforeseen benefits. It's making me more aware of natural conditions, of nature itself, and of the beauty of each day. Walking to the bus stop on Thursday morning, I notice a pink sunrise. That same day, coming home from the clinic, I see the rosy glow of a late afternoon sky. I would have missed these if I were still driving my car. I would have been preoccupied with driving.

And something else. Going carless is teaching me patience. To stand and wait, just a few minutes, in the past, was extremely difficult for me. Now it's getting easier.

Why is that? Perhaps it's because I often have company. Others are waiting with me. I am part of a community of riders. I'm part of what's happening today in my city. People going to work, moving about the city, living their lives.

And if I'm standing alone, I practice mindful breathing. Or intentionally relaxing my body. Or standing straighter. Once I arrive at a bus stop, I don't have to do anything at all, so my mind is free.

I'm amazed, in fact, how little I really miss my car. I don't miss the hassle of scraping off the windshield ice. Or filling it up with gas in below-zero weather. Or worrying about getting it started. Or parking it on the right streets in a snow emergency.

There's an art to getting out the door when you're a rider, and not a driver. Before, I'd dash out to the garage with almost no lead time at all. If I was running late, I could always drive faster. Now if I'm running late, I could miss one bus, and maybe two if my ride involves a transfer.

I need to pace the countdown to liftoff, so that I'm not dashing around like a madwoman before I leave, hastily grabbing the things I need. Now most of these things are in an African market basket by my front door. Scarves, hats, gloves, a collection of foldable totes, a water bottle, an energy bar. I call the basket my launching pad.

If I need these things, I have to carry them *on my person*. They can't be tucked away in a glove compartment or stashed on a back seat. But if I take too much stuff, it will add up to a heavy load that I won't be happy hauling around. So I need to choose carefully, taking what I need, but no more.

First, a sorting out process before I grab my purse and house keys. Then, a quick mental check-list: cash for bus fare, bus schedule, a library book to return, a package to mail. But I don't have to remember and find my car keys anymore! It's remarkable how liberating *that* feels.

Now I leave and come home through my front door—instead of driving into my garage and walking through the laundry into my kitchen. The front door is the entrance humans are meant to use. It's the way my 1926 house was designed. Coming in the front door, I'm greeted by the most pleasant space in my house, the living room, not the least pleasant, the laundry. It's a warm welcome that makes me surprisingly happy to be home.

Sunday morning, I walk to Dunn Bros to buy the *New York Times*. It's still cold—ten degrees below zero. I'm happy to come right home, make my own coffee, and settle in with the paper.

Midday, Nordis calls. "Do you want to see *Slum Dog Millionaire*?

"Sure!"

She picks me up and drives to a theater in Edina, the next suburb to the south. We stop to eat first and have a good chat. I consider paying for her movie ticket, but decide on buying her lunch instead. It felt right. Maybe I'm beginning to solve this ride-share puzzle.

I check out the MetroTransit website and try the "Plan My Trip" feature. It's easy. (Why didn't I try this sooner?) In seconds I have the routes and the times for customized trips. I need to get to St. Paul for a professional meeting later this week. It will take me two buses and about an hour, twice the time it would take to drive my car. Still, I can't beat the price. Midday and weekends: $1.75. Rush hour: $2.25 For seniors, it is even more of a bargain. Midday and weekends: only 75 cents. In just eighteen months, I'll be 65. But I wonder if I can last that long.

I find this experiment in carless living both a daily puzzle to solve. And an extreme sport. I have lived in Minnesota all my adult life and I have never been so exposed to the winter elements as I have this year. It is testing my fortitude. And my commitment.

I decide at the last minute to go to an evening class at House of Prayer in the City, a retreat center in downtown Minneapolis. I hop on a northbound #6 bus and get there just in time. I did not want to leave my warm house to catch a bus. But in winter, a city bus is a huge lumbering self-propelled box of warmth. As soon as I sit down, I'm removing my hat, my scarf, my mittens and reminding myself that it would have taken the whole ride downtown—about 15 minutes—for the inside of my car to warm up.

After class, I ask if anyone is going my way. Diane offers to take me home.

"But how did you *get* here?" she asks.

"I took the bus."

"The bus!!" She appears to be shocked that I would do such a thing. Alone. At night.

"My car is in storage. I'm experimenting with the carless life."

"Carless in Minneapolis—in the winter?!"

"Well, if I can do it in winter, I can probably do it year round."

"What got you to make the break? I mean, how were you able to give up your car?"

She is genuinely interested. Most of my friends

can't imagine life without their cars, but they love to hear what led to my experiment.

How *did* I get here?

In 1987, I wanted to drop one notch down on the food chain, so I simply stopped eating meat and poultry. I'd read Frances Moore Lappe's *Diet for a Small Planet* and one day, I made a quiet promise to myself to change my ways. I knew that one person's eating habits would not impact America's beef, pork and poultry industries, but I believed that somehow it would matter. And it was one thing I *could* do. So I did it. It was easier than I thought possible to just say no to meat.

In 1999, a year after my husband died, I made more changes when I left my corporate life to go to graduate school. I told myself, in order to self-fund my grad program, I was going to have to live like a grad student. Even though I was in my 50s then and didn't look anything like a grad student, I learned to live within a grad student's budget. I kept discretionary expenses to a minimum. I unplugged the TV cable connection. I bought all my clothes (except shoes and underwear) at consignment shops. I switched from department store cosmetics to lines I could get at the drug store. I used the public library more than I had in decades.

And I bought more used books than new ones. I favored reduced priced movie matinees and rush line theater tickets. And I discovered social dance, a new passion that met a lot of needs: to meet new friends, hear live music, keep physically active, have fun and learn a new skill, all very much on the cheap. With a $7 cover charge, a *milonga* (an Argentine tango dance party) cost less than a movie.

On the surface, my life did not look substantially different than it had. Nor did I. I still got my hair done at a salon. I still loved good food and good times with friends, but instead of restaurant dinners we went for happy hour only. Or for coffee. Or we ate in. We shared many a pot-luck meal at my house. I still drove my 2002 Subaru Forester. But as a grad student, with more time than money, I learned that, with a little creativity, I could cut back my spending significantly in almost every area of my life.

In 2002, having graduated with a masters in theology, I began part-time work as an Episcopal spiritual director. Spiritual counseling is personally rewarding work, but the income is as tiny as you might imagine. Now my primary sources of income are my social security check and a rent check from the tenants who live in my duplex home.

I'm still doing all the things that helped me get through school and I'm looking for one more thing to cut. Transportation is one big expense I have some control over. There is a part of it which I'm not willing to eliminate: airfares to see my family in Maryland, New York and California, but the car part of transportation is the big chunk I am willing to consider.

Americans spend an average of $750 a month on car ownership, including payments, fuel, maintenance, insurance—everything, including depreciation.[1] That's a huge piece of my discretionary spending. Plus, I ask myself, what's the most expensive thing I own that's losing value every day? Answer: My car.

When I add up the numbers, it's clear that my car is a luxury I can no longer afford.

But can I give it up entirely?

There are some things in my favor. I'm 63 and in good health. I live in a part of Minneapolis known as Uptown, where I can walk to grocery stores, coffee shops, cafes, bookshops and theaters. I live alone and need to buy groceries for only one person. I work part-time on a flexible schedule. I don't have to commute to work. My clients come to my home. When I need to get around town, a major bus line is a block away.

Yet this change feels like it is going to be the hardest one yet. If I'm to keep it up for the long haul, it's going to challenge me in many ways. Minneapolis—like most American cities—is not known for its excellent public transportation system. And its weather is not for sissies.

Shifting to a carless lifestyle is a tricky business in America, because our society is built around cars. Most American cities, and especially their suburbs, have been designed for drivers, not walkers. To live without a car in America seems downright counter-cultural.

And yet…and yet, there are cities in America where people thrive without cars. There's New York City, where my younger son and his family happily live without one. Washington, D.C., San Francisco, Boston, and Portland are also friendly to the carless. Outside the U.S., there are countless places where people live perfectly well without cars. In fact, only 15% of the world's population owns cars. More than 75% of the U.S. population owns cars.[2] It turns out that going carless is counter-cultural *only* in America.

And there are plenty of good reasons to go carless, over and above the financial ones. The biggest impact most people can have on their carbon footprint, on a daily basis, is to stop driving. And, although, the world's environmental problems often seem overwhelming and complex, giving up my car is something simple and positive that I can do. Simple, maybe, but not exactly easy.

All I can do is try.

Last night I was determined to use the bus to get to a friend's party. I carefully checked the schedules and found I could get *near* his house if I took two buses. But—first mistake!—I wore clothes that were appropriate for a party, but not for bussing on a winter night. No storm boots, no long underwear, a light weight scarf and dress gloves.

To make matters worse, the bus drove right by me. It must have been because I was wearing all black, and my bus stop was poorly lit. I waited 25 minutes in the cold and dark for the next bus, which was not the right one. But because I was so cold, I jumped on it. Second mistake! It took me nine blocks off course.

I ended up walking the nine blocks back to where the right bus would have been dropped me off, plus *eleven more* blocks, to get to the party. I got there more than an hour after I'd set out. A cab ride would have been all of 10 minutes.

Miserable, I trudged along a busy city thoroughfare, in the dark, on icy sidewalks and through dirty slush at every curb, hoping in vain to catch a connecting bus, which ran only every half hour. I learned a hard lesson: at night, if my destination is not on a major bus route, take a cab.

MetroTransit has a convenient electronic card system. There's no muss, no fuss with coins and dollar bills. It's infinitely re-usable. You just top it off online with a credit card. But I haven't ordered one yet. I'm still paying cash for each ride. I think buying the green plastic Go-To Card is like joining a club. I think of it as a symbol of my commitment to this new way of doing things. I'm not quite ready to join the club.

It's still cold and windy this morning. I bundle up and take the 7:30 northbound #6 to the Cathedral. This bus fills up quickly with hip young professionals from Uptown who are heading downtown, iPods and iPhones everywhere. I wonder how many of them have cars that they choose *not* to drive downtown. Maybe most of them. These are the discretionary bus riders, who have figured out it's just smarter to ride the bus downtown than to drive. Cheaper. Easier. Greener. You can chill for the first (and last) half hour of your work day instead of fighting traffic.

I chill with them.

Late one afternoon a young man gets on the bus. He's tall, pale and rail thin. He takes an unusually long time to pay his fare. He stands by the driver, digging for coins in his cargo pants pocket. He seems confused. The portly, white-haired bus driver waits patiently. The young man finally scoops up all the loose change in his pockets and tosses the coins in the coin box, not counting them. They make a loud racket going through the box. It seems like a lot, but he comes up a dime short.

He looks at the other passengers and asks no one in particular, "Does anyone have a dime?" I'm the person sitting closest to him. I fish out some coins from my wallet. I have a quarter, so I hand it to him. He takes it and drops it in.

The driver ribs him gently: "Now you have credit." We all smile. The young man moves to the back of the bus.

Now the bus driver gets up from his seat and bends down on one knee with some difficulty—he is no longer young—to loosen the double security straps on not one but two electric wheelchairs for two disabled passengers. The pair seem to be husband and wife. They both appear to have cerebral palsy. The driver skillfully unstraps their chairs, returns to his seat, and lowers the automatic step for each wheelchair passenger to de-board, painstakingly, one at a time. They buzz on down the sidewalk in their chairs. I am no longer young, either, but if these two are able to ride the bus in the cold and the growing darkness, then shouldn't I be willing?

Bus riding is opening up to me a fascinating parallel universe of human interaction that I was totally missing when I drove my own car. Without realizing it, I've been driving around in my own four-wheeled "isolation booth." Now I'm just beginning to get a glimpse of something larger. And it has my attention. I'm watching with beginner's eyes.

I'm teaching myself the art of waiting. At a bus stop, I stand and breathe. I consciously relax my body. I've learned not to strain to see if the bus is coming, willing it to show up by steadily peering down the street for it. That doesn't help. The bus will come when it comes. I have no power to make it arrive one minute sooner. So I relax.

Once on the bus, I'm happy to be warm, to be sitting, to be moving steadily in the right direction, with absolutely no effort on my part. I sit back and let the driver do all the work. My only job is to show up.

When I was running late in my car, I would push to make up the time, driving faster than usual, eyes on the speedometer, pushing the speed limit, looking for openings, changing lanes, passing slower cars, running yellow lights as they turned red, barely pausing at stop signs, all in order to get to wherever I was going a few minutes sooner. I was often full of tension—barely breathing, white-knuckling the steering wheel, getting more agitated and irritable by the minute. I could blame my irritability on the traffic or the weather, but really I was mad at myself for not paying more attention to the time before I left the house.

Now, as a bus rider, it's another world. If I'm running late now, there's nothing I can do to catch up. The steering wheel is literally out of my hands. The driver doesn't care about my schedule. And suddenly it doesn't matter as much to me, either. I let myself be late without judgment. Amazingly, I relax.

It's remarkable how good it feels to stop pushing the river.

A man at my coffee shop once told me if he were rich, the only thing he'd want different in his life would be someone to drive him around, so he could just sit back and relax. Now I've got the rich man's privilege of having someone to drive me around.

Valentine's Day. The Tango Society of Minnesota is celebrating its tenth anniversary, with a special *milonga* in St. Paul. Taking a cab is out of the question. It's much too far. So, I arrange a ride with fellow *tangueros*, Steve and Sandra.

Sandra says she lived happily without a car in Tokyo when her two boys were very young. She felt "liberated" to be able to bike around town on an old-fashioned Schwinn-type bicycle, carting groceries and two tots.

Steve and Sandra totally endorse my project, saying, "This is a lifestyle change." They're right. This is more than changing a habit. Much more. I happily give them $10 for the ride, but their encouragement is priceless.

"Give it away, if you don't want to keep it for yourself," I say. This is getting to be my standard phrase as I pass my friends a bill, $5 for shorter rides, $10 for longer ones. My carless project is allowing others to give and receive—or give again.

I don't go to contemplative prayer at the Cathedral this

morning. I'm not happy about that. I hardly ever miss, unless I'm out of town, but I can't be sure of getting back by bus in time for a 9:00 appointment in Uptown. I would have been fine, zipping back in my car, but not on a bus.

Another lesson: Don't schedule my day too tightly. Living without a car is training me to leave breathing room between the things I plan to do.

I bus downtown to my Monday evening class. On this cold, dark night I really don't want to leave my house and wait for a bus on a deserted street corner. 20 degrees is not that cold, but the air is damp and I am feeling chilled. Why am I doing this crazy carless thing? What's the point?

Then I see a small figure slowly approaching the corner stop. He is shorter than the average kindergartener, bent over, knock-kneed. He walks awkwardly, with a lop-sided gait. He stops every thirty feet or so and leans against a shop window. He coughs deeply, catching his breath. As he approaches, I realize he is carrying a portable oxygen tank on his back and wears a tube in his nose. His mouth stays open slightly. He seems to be missing more teeth than he has retained. As he reaches me, he speaks with extra politeness, not waiting for me to greet him. "Good evening, Ma'am." Two minutes later, as the bus approaches and we both move toward it, he says, "You first, Ma'am."

This man snaps me out of my whiney mood. If he can be riding a bus on a night like this, struggling with each step, fighting for each breath, surely I can, too. It seems worth doing again.

I get a call from Al, the man who is storing my car. He likes it. He wants to buy it. I surprise myself by starting to negotiate the sale of my car. He will get back to me in a day or two with an offer.

If anyone asks what I am giving up for Lent, I can say: I'm giving up my car.

I walk to Dunn Bros for coffee at 10:00. The morning is exquisitely beautiful. New snow is piled up everywhere. And I am supremely happy not to have a car today! No scraping ice off the windshield. No worrying if the car will start and if it starts, no struggling to get it out of the snow. No waiting for it to warm up or driving in a large moving icebox.

I feel free.

I tell my coffee shop buddies that. They look dubious. Rick is coveting a new car he saw on-line. He'd rather talk about that.

I walk to Lunds after coffee and come home with two bags full of groceries—a little workout that's getting easier day by day. Am I getting stronger? Maybe. One thing for sure: I'm getting my share of fresh air, sunshine and Vitamin D.

Rick says having a car gives him freedom. I don't deny that. But what kind of freedom? We're thinking about two different kinds. He's thinking about freedom to go anywhere, any time.

I'm thinking about freedom from car payments, insurance bills, car tags and license plates, pumping gas, watching the gas gauge and the gas prices, keeping my car serviced and maintained. I'm talking about freedom from unexpected repair bills and the hassle of getting the repairs accomplished. Freedom from worrying about a possible fender bender—or worse. Freedom from the trouble and expense to repair or replace the car, not to mention any physical damage to myself or others. Freedom from hunting for parking spaces in the city and then paying for them. Freedom from the aggravation of moving the car to the right streets on the right days during a snow emergency, and the threat of an expensive towing fee if I don't.

I'm starting to realize there is a built-in, low-level stress to driving that we generally discount because it is so common in our culture. It's like breathing at higher altitudes—everyone does it—but there is an easier way. Go to a lower elevation.

When I'm riding a bus, my mind can drift anywhere at all. I don't spend mental energy and adrenaline on calculating whether I can slip through a yellow-turning-to-red light or whether I can pass the car in front before the oncoming truck zips by.

My kind of freedom is starting to stack up for me.

I now have 23 bus transfer tickets in a bowl on my kitchen counter. I've been saving them, souvenirs of the last two months' rides. Actually, it's more than 23 rides. Each transfer represents two or more rides. And most of my rides didn't require a transfer. Whatever the number, it's more bus rides than I've taken in the whole rest of my life.

What does it take to change a life-long habit? The car habit is a tough one to kick in this culture, but I may be close. Can I make this more than a project? Is it possible that my new carless patterns will change *me*? So that soon I'll find myself happily in a new way of life?

I decide to go online and order the MetroTransit GoTo Card, choosing the $40 denomination which gives me a 10% discount. I'm joining the club.

LIST 1: THINGS TO DO ON A BUS, SUBWAY OR TRAIN
(requiring no equipment)

1. Take a break. Relax.

2. Watch your city go by.

3. People watch. You never know what you'll see on the next bus ride.

4. People listen. Conversations among riders are the best reality show in town.

5. Join in the conversation, if you feel like it.

6. Get to know the person sitting next to you.

7. Breathe deeply.

8. Close your eyes. Doze, even.

9. Meditate.

10. Say a mantra: "Peace" or "Love" or "You have more time than you think."

11. Count your blessings.

12. Say a blessing: for your day, or for those around you, or for beloved absent ones.

13. Pray.

14. Daydream.

15. Ponder a dilemma or solve a problem, or just sit with it quietly and let a solution surface on its own.

LIST 2: THINGS TO DO ON A BUS, SUBWAY OR TRAIN
(requiring low-tech equipment)

1. Read.
2. Make notes to yourself.
3. Make shopping lists.
4. Memorize something. A poem, a prayer, lyrics to a song.
5. Study for a test.
6. Learn new words in your own language or in someone else's.

LIST 3: THINGS TO DO ON A BUS, SUBWAY OR TRAIN
(requiring a personal electronic device)

1. Call home. Call work. Call your kids.

2. Check your email.

3. Check the weather, the stock market, news headlines, or your favorite columnist.

4. Text a friend, lover, kid.

5. Listen to your favorite music (on earphones).

6. Listen to a great lecture, a speech, a poem (on earphones).

7. Read a book for work, school or pleasure (on a pad).

LIST 4: BE A RIDER IN THE KNOW

Mass transit riding is a team sport. Smart riders know how to play.

1. Wait for any departing passengers to get off first, then step on board.

2. Have your money, transfer or transit card ready when you board. Don't take forever to find it, while people behind you wait to board.

3. Give up your seat for disabled riders, elders and parents with squirrelly, over-tired youngsters.

4. When it's gets crowded, don't take up more than one seat. Consolidate your parcels.

5. Keep your cell phone voice down.

6. Get up and move toward the door when you're near your stop, so your driver doesn't have to wait for you.

7. Look back at your seat as you leave, to see if you left anything behind.

8. Thank your drivers. Praise them once in a while. They are doing a difficult job.

LIST 5: THINGS TO DO WHILE WAITING FOR A BUS

1. Relax. You can't make it come sooner by leaning over the curb and straining to see it, so relax.

2. Breathe deeply.

3. Check in with your body. Notice your posture. Adjust it, if necessary. Align your bones for maximum height. Relax your muscles.

4. Check in with your mind. Notice your mental posture. Are you weary, rushing, anxious, calm, sunny or blue? Adjust your attitude, if necessary.

5. If others are waiting with you, and you feel like it, chat with one of them. You'll almost never regret it, especially if the wait is going to be more than five minutes. The time goes much faster when you have a little company.

6. If no one else is there with you, you can hum, whistle, or sing.

7. When the bus is about to arrive, step up to the curb, but not on the curb. Be visible to the driver, but don't risk life or limb.

Riding west on the #23 bus, I see a thin middle-aged man with a large roller suitcase and a bulging blue plastic bag struggle to get up the bus steps, pay his fare, and take his seat. He looks tired and worn. He apparently is hauling his possessions in the only moving van he can afford. Has he been evicted from his place? Does he have a place to go now?

He is clearly in distress. He talks non-stop in a low monotone, to no one in particular. I gather that the suitcase is a gift from his new brother-in-law. "God provides," the man says. His new brother-in-law is "a good man." Not like his former brother-in-law. His former brother-in-law is "an evil man." He got into a fight with his sister when she was six months pregnant. He punched her in the stomach. She started to miscarry at home...and she had the baby in the bathtub. The brother-in-law "pulled the baby out," and put it in a garbage bag, and put the bag in a dumpster.

Is this a true story? I don't know, but it has the ring of truth.

The man goes on. The "evil" brother-in-law got him drunk one night and beat him up with a broken beer bottle. The man was saved by a friend. "God provides," he repeats.

The man gets off the bus, but his story hangs in the air.

I'm riding the southbound #6 to Uptown. An older man is sitting in the "talking seat," the first seat across from the driver. He's got a bushy gray beard and thick glasses. Both hands are resting on a cane, planted firmly between his legs. He leans into it as he talks to the driver. He's complaining loudly and at length about many things—the economy, local politicians, pot-holes in the street. He's just a bitter old guy, I think, spewing venom, spreading it around, spraying a thin film of nastiness on everyone within earshot.

I have just read about the Buddhist practice called *metta*, where you pray for someone who is causing you or others some harm. You pray for their happiness.

I decide to try it. With this stranger across the aisle from me in mind, I pray: "May he be happy. May his heart be open. May he find contentment and peace."

I wait. He doesn't stop complaining, but *I feel better...* which is, I think, the point of the practice.

Then, a surprising thing happens. He stops talking and reaches for a bus schedule tucked in a small dispenser high above his head. He makes several attempts to pull one down—with his cane!—but it isn't going well.

Then, the teenager sitting next to him hops up, grabs a schedule and hands it to the man in a friendly, natural way. He simply takes his seat again. Side by side, the old man and the youth exchange a few pleasantries. In that moment, there is contentment and peace.

It's still quite cold. It feels worse, somehow, because there's more moisture in the air. I feel it, because I'm out in it. I take a #6 bus to 22nd and Hennepin and then walk five blocks to my spiritual director's home. I tell her about the ups and down of my carless project, the cold and the weariness, about the people I'm encountering, the way they're expanding my heart. It's out of my comfort zone in so many ways. Is this a fool's errand, especially at my age? Could I be doing something better with my time and energy? What is this experiment teaching me? I try to sort it out with her. It helps to be listened to so deeply.

As I'm riding the 7:30 #6 bus, heading for the Cathedral, two young Somali women in head scarves, long silk skirts, parkas and backpacks, are chatting very quietly—almost whispering—in their native tongue. Three of four student types nearby are reading books, noses buried in their private worlds. Others are pensively readying themselves for another workday, aluminum travel mugs of coffee in mittened hands. There is intentional group silence on this bus, a contemplative community on wheels.

I lead the contemplative prayer service at the Cathedral at 8:00. Afterwards, I walk to the Dunn Bros coffee shop in Loring Park for a chat with my good friends from the Cathedral group.

I hop onto another downtown bus to check out a sale at Macy's. And then, it's time to walk four blocks to Westminster Presbyterian Church, for a Town Hall Forum lecture by Dr. Barbara Brown Taylor. Her talk is called "The Art of Sacred Down Time." "Sacred down time" is an accurate description of what is happening in my life. More "sacred down time" is being slipped into every day, walking to and from the bus stops, waiting for and riding on the buses. I have time to notice the day, time to relax and breathe deeply, time to be in a quietly receptive mode. The reward for practicing this art is a new feeling of spaciousness in my life.

My friend Nordis has a dream to walk the ancient pilgrimage to Santiago de Compostela, in northern Spain. There are many routes of different lengths, but the major route, from a town near Biarritz, France is almost 500 miles long and involves 20 or 30 days of walking. It makes her happy to think of training for it, building up her stamina, and being able to join other pilgrims on that ancient route. She says, "It would be a lifetime achievement."

What makes me happy is to integrate walking into my everyday life—with no great destination, no great goal, except to be stay fit enough to live without a car. Not exactly a lifetime achievement, but something.

On a Saturday morning, the eastbound #23 bus is not full. But what it lacks in numbers, it makes up for in diversity. A few Hispanic men and women coming from or going to work, wearing hospital scrubs under their parkas. Some young people, of mixed ethnic heritage— black, white and brown—but with a unified sense of teen fashion. Boys with baggy jeans dragging well below their jackets. The goal apparently is to show some underwear to teen girls. How do they keep their pants up, anyway? And girls in skin tight jeans. The goal here is obvious. But how do they get into them?

A group of developmentally challenged adults board the bus with their social worker. They appear to be on a special outing. Excited, they talk animately to each other and sometimes to themselves.

I notice one middle-aged woman sitting slightly apart from her group. Her hair is blond, wispy, and disheveled. She wears a man's purple-and-gold knit cap with a Vikings emblem on it. Her lower jaw sticks out. Her lips are pursed, caved in. She has no teeth.

The woman tips her head at an odd angle to see through her thick glasses and looks around. When she catches my eye, I look at her directly and smile.

Her face breaks out into the widest, brightest, purest smile! Is it for me? Yes, I think it must be.

Tonight there is an Argentine tango event at a downtown studio. I want to dress "dance appropriate," and I don't relish the idea of standing in the cold at a bus stop on a Saturday night.

I call a cab. It's on time—and it's warm. The driver is friendly. The ride is fast and costs me $10, including the tip. I feel ridiculously happy with my decision. And something of a celebrity. My limo is a Green & White taxi. My chauffeur is a handsome young Somalian. It doesn't matter that it's dark and cold and quite late. I simply pay my driver, hop out and walk a few steps into the warm, inviting ambience of a *milonga* in progress.

Al, the man who is storing my car, wants to buy it. Friday I gave him my price: $9500. He counter-offered with $8500. I told him I'd think about it. Over the weekend I call my two sons.

"Should I sell it? And if so, at what price?"

My New York son says, "Sure, sell it. But haggle."

My California son says, "If you can get $500 less than Blue Book, go for it."

But by Sunday, I have a little complication. My friend Susan says she may want to buy it. Her car, a 12-year-old Saturn, is in the shop with a pothole injury, and she doesn't know if her mechanic will advise her to dump it or not.

"Can you wait one day? He's getting back to me Monday morning."

"Of course."

On Monday morning, Susan calls. She's keeping her car. She's going to try to get one more year out of it. It's a recession, after all.

Monday afternoon, I check Kelly Blue Book again to review the Private Party Value for my car: it's $10,110 for excellent condition, $9,535 for good. I think my car is somewhere between excellent and good, with low mileage for its age.

I decide I'll be happy with $9000 or more. But not less.

I call Al. "Would you want my car for $9200?"

"Yes," he answers without skipping a beat.

"OK. I guess we've got a deal."

This is easy! Maybe too easy? This guy knows cars. Does he know something I don't?

I start to get all the documents together for him and I discover that I have looked up the value of the *wrong model*. Turns out, mine is actually valued at $10,945 in excellent condition and $10,345 in good condition.

But I have no regrets. Al will get the car he wants at a really good price! I'll get a quick and easy sale to a cash customer in a recession. This is a good deal for both of us.

Riding on an unfamiliar bus line is a minor adventure. As I'm leaving downtown Minneapolis on the #16 going east to St. Paul, it gives me a strange feeling to pass by buildings that are part of my personal history—The Loft Literary Center, Metro Stadium, University West Bank and University Main Campus—and to see them with new eyes. My eyes are new because, for the first time, I don't need to keep them on the road. I'm suddenly a tourist in a town I've lived in for forty years.

I see the people of my town with new eyes as well. Bus riders come in all sizes, shapes, and colors. I see earnest young students—white, black, Asian, Hispanic, the global blend—heading for class. As we leave the campus and head east to the Midway section of St. Paul, I see rowdy young teens and older men with canes. Were these old men the young rowdies once? Are they Vietnam vets, now our walking wounded?

I see sadness. A tall young woman hugs a stocky young man who has just told her something that brings *him* to tears.

I see happiness. A teen seems thrilled to meet his friend at the bus stop. He apparently needs money for the fare. His friend hands him the cash. The smile on his face is an "I just won the lottery!" smile.

I see compassion. A bus driver helps an elderly woman who is desperate, lost and confused. She needs to get to a Minneapolis hospital. "I just want to see my brother," she says plaintively over and over. But she is on a bus going in the opposite direction. The driver gives her a six-hour day pass. He carefully explains how and where to catch the bus she needs. He does it twice. And then once more.

I see tenderness. Two young people are holding hands and talking softly to each other. At their stop, the young man helps his companion off the bus. She is crippled and uses crutches.

I see strength and grit. Two poor young moms with bundled-up babes and toddlers, manage to board the bus with strollers and parcels and settle their kids in for the ride.

I see romance. Two attractive teens are flirting outrageously. They smile and laugh, delighted by each others' comments, as if they were in their own private world. They are. They both carry the long white sticks of the blind.

A wide range of human emotions and conditions are on display for anyone to see. Riding a bus is more than an adventure, it is a heart-expanding spiritual exercise.

Al gets my car out of cold storage—his specialty garage for classic cars—and drives it to my house. There it is. I haven't seen it for two months. It looks great. But the deal is done. It's not my car anymore. It feels strange to retrieve my personal stuff from the cargo areas and toss it into a cardboard box. Like somebody died.

Al has a bill of sale made up. And a personal check. I have the title. He has written the check for $100 *more* than the price we negotiated. I point that out to him, but he seems fine with it. I am pleased, too. It's a sweet gesture on his part, a bit of icing on the cake.

I tell him I'd like to take a photo.

"Sure thing," he says.

Click. Click.

"Got it. Thanks."

He drives away.

I can't watch. When I can bring myself to look out the window, I still see the ghost image of the car that was there a minute ago, but the street is empty.

Nothing else to do but sort through the stuff in the box. There's an outdated Rand McNally Road Atlas and half a dozen fold-out road maps, a *Wildflowers of Minnesota Guidebook*, 2 Spanish language CDs, 2 blue IKEA tote bags, a small yellow tool box, a large hazard flashlight that doesn't work, a AAA sticker, an insurance card, a few old church bulletins, a long-handled windshield scraper and snow brush.

It occurs to me that most of these things I may never need again. And suddenly I feel much lighter, less encumbered.

I get a ride to and from St. Paul for a professional meeting with Bob, another spiritual director. I give him $10 for car fare, which he refuses to take at first, but I tell him, "If you don't want to keep it, then give it to your favorite charity or the next homeless person you meet." He accepts it with a smile.

In the evening, I get a ride to and from a *milonga* downtown from a tango friend. I cheerfully hand him my car fare. It's starting to feel normal—not having wheels myself but getting rides from friends who do. I'm happy to pay them because I want to be able to ask them again. They seem to want to help me out and don't mind getting the extra money for gas. We all agree that one less car on the road is a good thing. It's working.

LIST 6: WHAT TO DO
WHEN RIDE-SHARING

1. Call ahead when asking for a ride. Give your friends several days advance warning. If you wait until the day you need a ride, it will appear to be an emergency. No one appreciates that kind of subtle pressure, not even your best friends.

2. Always let your friends know you have other options. You do.

3. Be ready at the appointed time, waiting near the front door and watching for your ride. Never make them wait for you.

4. Be willing to leave your event whenever your friends say they want to leave. This is not something to negotiate! Put yourself on their schedule. Go with their flow.

5. Be quick about getting ready to go. Don't even think about making them wait while you finish a "little" conversation with someone else. On the other hand, be patient if your friends choose to take a little longer themselves.

6. Enjoy your friends' company! Listen to their stories (and their soundtracks)! Take this opportunity to get to know them a little better.

7. Don't drown them in the details of your day. Notice when the road is going to demand their full attention, and simply put your story on "pause."

8. Be patient with extra stops your driver may need to make.

9. Give them carfare—something in return for their help. My general rule is $5 for an in-town trip, $10 for a cross-town or suburban trip. This is far cheaper than a taxi and it will be appreciated, no matter what people say. I try to keep bills in those denominations in my wallet at all times. And before the ride, I put them in my coat pocket for easy access. That way, I'm not fishing in my wallet for the right bills, or suddenly realizing I don't have the right bills.

10. When you give money to your friends, don't just offer. Gently insist. Be prepared to tell them, "By doing this, you are keeping one car off the road. You are helping the world go greener. If you don't feel comfortable keeping this, then give it away to the next person who needs it more than you do." And leave the money on the seat.

11. If cash doesn't seem right, find another way to pay them. Pay for parking or their movie ticket, their glass of wine, or their cover charge.

12. If it seems appropriate, offer to barter a comparable service. I've bartered marketing consulting. Help with a garden. Advice about paint colors and furniture and art placement.

LIST 7: WHAT NOT TO DO WHEN RIDE-SHARING

1. Don't be a backseat driver. Don't say a word about their driving habits. If you aren't comfortable with the way they drive, don't ask them to drive you again.

2. Never give directions, unless they're specifically requested. And don't tell them the route you usually take. They may prefer a completely different route that is equally good.

3. Don't forget that you are not in the driver's seat anymore. Practice surrendering that role every time you ride with someone.

I walk to Dunn Bros and share my "no car" news with Rick, who just bought one. We are both happy! I'm thrilled to be free of mine. He's thrilled to have acquired a new used car, one "nicer than I've ever had in my life," he says. He's tickled, like a kid who got the best birthday present ever. I can see his pleasure. He takes me outside the shop to show me his new prize. I'm really happy for him. And I think he's genuinely happy for me.

It's a rainy Sunday, not pouring, just overcast and drizzly. I intend to bus to my church for the 9:00 service and the adult education hour at 10:00, but I'm late by a few minutes and miss my bus, so I go home to wait for about 20 minutes. Then, I try again, catching the next bus, and end up coming into the last part of the early service. I stay for the education hour and the first part of the late service. And then I leave. It's a little odd, but it works.

Then, on the same fare, I take a bus downtown to Orchestra Hall for a 12:30 dress rehearsal with famed choral composer Eric Whitacre, conducting his own work. It's a marvelous experience listening to 360 singers with a full orchestra perform this dynamic, ethereal composition.

Afterward, walking along Nicollet Avenue is a treat. Spring is actually here. The air is mild and fresh. And I'm pleased to be taking in my city at a walker's pace.

It's in the mid-forties today, rainy and windy. Waiting more than ten minutes for a bus, in the rain and the wind, isn't fun. I am headed for a massage across town. This is not a good way to get there. I almost walk away, back to my warm, dry house.

On the way home, the westbound #23 bus is late. I wait more than ten minutes *again*, and, if anything, it's windier and colder now. I recall how easy it used to be to drive. It took me ten minutes flat, each way. Today, a half an hour, each way.

I could take a cab both ways, save time and avoid the hassle, but cab rides, at perhaps $15 each, would be an ongoing expense that I can't justify.

After church today I stop at a favorite yarn shop, but then there is a chilly wait of about 20 minutes for the next bus. I forgot. Sunday afternoon isn't the best time for bussing. On this route, they run only every half hour. But I'm beginning to wonder if being outside on these cold days could actually be healthy for me. Because I walk more, I feel my body more. I notice if I'm weary or not, and I pace myself accordingly. What a concept! Pacing myself to my body's abilities. Could functioning in this slower rhythm of "walk—wait—ride," living in the not-so-fast-lane, actually be good for me?

I catch the #6 bus to contemplative prayer at the Cathedral. It's my new normal. I don't check the schedule. I just go. I leave my house only ten minutes earlier that I used to leave when I drove there. That's all. It's remarkable.

Mother's Day. I'm going with my friend Nordis to the Eloise Butler Wildflower Garden, a small wooded glen in the heart of the city. She picks me up. The day is clear, but none too warm. Trillium and other tender spring woodland flowers are in abundance. We two moms, with grown kids on both coasts, enjoy our quiet walk and reminisce about earlier Mother's Days here. I treat her to brunch and she drives me home.

Sometimes, my friends take routes I'm not familiar with. They take me into pockets of my city that are all new to me, all fresh, just minutes from my former routes.

I didn't realize how many habitual patterns I was in, the deep grooves of my own making, until I was suddenly not in them anymore.

I do a few errands in Uptown, including an exploratory visit to Calhoun Cycle, a neighborhood bike shop. I want to know: "How much for a bike rack and two side baskets?" The shop owner says, "The rack, the baskets and the installation, $120." The "baskets" are actually sturdy black nylon totes, the shape of grocery bags. I like them. I need a seasonal tune-up, too. I decide I'll invest in my bicycle, which has now become the only vehicle I own. I'll make it road-worthy for doing errands.

It turns out, one of the secret pleasures of riding the bus is imagining the lives of the other riders. We riders do it all the time.

One weekday afternoon on a suburban bus heading back into the city, I see a young father with his two preschool boys on the side seats in front. The man is dressed casually, Banana Republic-style. His older son has a cute kid-style mohawk and cool shoes. The little guy is bright-eyed and inquisitive. He asks one question after another. His father quietly answers each one, patiently, seriously. Among other things, the boy wants to know if they could go fishing at his grandmother's. And if they went fishing, would they catch any. And if they caught some fish, could they clean them and cook them and eat the fish for dinner. The younger boy, snuggled in close to his dad, says not a word, but listens intently.

Clearly, this is a day trip. There are no backpacks and no fishing gear. I wonder, where is the mother? Is she at work? Is he a work-at-home dad, taking a break? Or is he perhaps out of work? They seem well off. Why did they choose to ride the bus? Do they have a car or maybe two, like many suburban families? Was this the boys' idea of an adventure or, have they sold one car to make ends meet? Is this ride to Grandma's a special treat or is it a new routine? Will she babysit for them, to help them get through a rough patch?

I won't ever know, but I can make up my own scenario.

My neighbor Toni picks me up at 12:30. We have the same chiropractor, but his office is in Golden Valley, a suburb to the west which is hard for me to get to, so we coordinate our appointments. She waits for me, while I have my session. I wait for her, while she has hers. We enjoy our chats, coming and going.

She tells me she is thoroughly pleased with her new Toyota Prius. "The mileage is amazing."

I think to myself. I'm thoroughly pleased having no car at all. But I can't do it alone. I need friends like Toni who still drive and who are willing to extend themselves on my behalf.

Midday, I try taking an eastbound #23 bus to St. Paul for a professional meeting. On this route, there are two construction detours which slow everything down. Construction is everywhere now. In Minnesota they say we have two seasons: winter and road construction. I'm sure I'm going to be late.

I tell my driver that I need to catch a connecting #74 bus. Just then, he sees a #74 bus pull up in front of him. He honks, LOUD and LONG. The #74 bus doesn't pull away. It waits! I jump off one and hop on the other. The timing couldn't have been closer. Amazingly, I make it to my meeting on time...through the courtesy and quick reflexes of two bus drivers.

Saturday evening, I call Jim, a friend who loves Argentine tango but who occasionally brakes for salsa.

"Want to go salsa dancing tonight?"

"Love to," he says.

"Can you pick me up?"

"Sure thing."

By 9:30, we're at Picosa, a downtown restaurant by the River that features live Cuban music. Jim tells me today is his birthday. Who knew? Not I. We dance and reminisce about the local places we've danced in over the last decade.

It was *una noche preciosa*, celebratory and poignant as well, because, as it turns out, his birthday falls on the same day my husband died, eleven years ago: May 16. Dance, more than anything, drew me out of grief, back into life.

We are all interconnected on many levels, but our normal American life does not tend to acknowledge or foster it. Our car-based lifestyle sometimes does just the opposite. Riding around in our own cars can isolate us and keep us from connecting. Even more important, it can lead us to believe that we are completely independent and self-sufficient, which we are not.

Now, without a car, interconnection is my way of life. I'm often dependent on others for rides. Usually, I can reciprocate with some payment, service, or favor. Often, though, the rides become more than a simple bartering experience. They become opportunities to talk longer, to deepen our connections.

The day is heating up—for the first time this year. I need to rest a bit on the way home from the grocery, putting down my shopping bags from time to time. The rest stops slow me down, but they also allow me to really appreciate the day. The tall elms and other boulevard trees are leafing out. A fine canopy of spring green stretches overhead. I stand up straight, breathe, notice.

Living carlessly is teaching me more than new shopping habits. It's teaching me to slow down. To accept my limitations. To go only as far and as fast as my body will allow. And to find the beauty along the way.

In her beautiful book of wisdom, *The Seven Whispers*, Christina Baldwin urges us to slow down and "move at the pace of guidance." Is this what she means?

At dinner time, I realize I'm out of mayonnaise. And it feels like too much effort to go to the store for just one ingredient. With my new "buy only what you can carry" mantra, I have put a jar of mayonnaise back on the grocery store shelf several times, because my basket was full.

What to do? Somewhere in the deep recesses of my brain, I have a faint image of Julia Child making mayonnaise with a big copper bowl and a wire whisk. I look up mayonnaise in my *Joy of Cooking* and find I have all the ingredients I need to make it. So I do. It's amazingly easy, fast, and delicious!

This feels like striking gold. I feel empowered somehow. From now on, my mayonnaise will be made from scratch because—in my new life—it's easier to make it than it is to lug it home from the store.

My first grocery shopping trip on my bicycle. I pull my bike up to the racks behind the store, lock it, unfasten both totes, take off my helmet, and stash my helmet and the totes in a grocery cart.

Even the young check-out guy is impressed with

them. "H-m-m. Cool," he says, as he unfolds a tote to fill it. He packs for equal weight in each tote. This is great! I buy a whole sack of potatoes this time, instead of just two or three potatoes. I buy more than I could carry on my own.

The biggest challenge is working the heavy bike lock. And I feel only slightly ridiculous in my helmet.

On the way home I have a little trouble balancing on the hill in the last block. All this is out of my comfort zone, but I tell myself, this will get easier with practice. Everything does.

Memorial Day. In the morning my friend Sallie picks me up so we can go to our favorite garden center together. She brings me and my plants back to my house.

Later in the afternoon, I bike to her house. It's a great day for a bike ride. Perfect, really. I love the Memorial Day scene by Lake Calhoun—families gathered on picnic blankets in the grass, dogs, babies, young people. The gardens lining the streets are beautiful. In minutes, I am at her house.

She shows me her garden and the plans she has for it. We have a little supper. We take our time and, before we know it, the sun is down. I'm not equipped for bike riding in the dark. I hadn't thought of that! She offers to take me and my bike home. I feel indebted to her for her driving today, but I don't offer money. Instead, I offer to stay overnight with her son David when she goes on a business trip next week. And she accepts.

A friendship deepens with proffered help that is really needed. It feels good, satisfying a desire I didn't know I had.

A #23 bus ride to my massage therapist turns out to be longer than planned because of two detours, in different places than the last time. This time I need to walk south four long blocks to get to her studio. I arrive huffing and puffing and ten minutes late.

Afterwards I decide to walk east eight short blocks to catch the light rail instead. It's about the same distance, but now I'm *choosing* to walk it, at my own pace, so it's not so bad. It's a quick and easy shot downtown from the 38th Street station to Nicollet Avenue, and just one block from there to the Central Library. I pick up two DVDs and then I take the #6 bus home. It's the long way home, but it's somehow more agreeable.

Still, I realize that my trips to get a massage are the most unpleasant part of my carless life. They nearly cancel the good that my massages do. My therapist is excellent and I have been with her for ten years. I would hate to leave her, but I have to admit this is not working. I could look for a new massage therapist closer to home. But, am I ready for one more change?

Midday, I walk to Lunds for groceries. The day is lovely. The air is satin smooth. Who wouldn't want to walk a few blocks on a day like this? Neighborhood gardens are bursting with flower and fragrance. And yet I know, if I had a car, I wouldn't be walking. I'd be zipping around town, inventing errands, and missing most of the beauty of this fine day.

I walk a block to Dunn Bros to pick up a Sunday *New York Times* and chat with some neighbors, who are sitting outside at cafe tables. I read the paper on my summer porch. I garden the rest of the afternoon. Later, I bike to the grocery store. It's a thoroughly beautiful outdoor day. I'm content to move in circles no wider than my feet and my bike can take me.

Tuesday on my way home from Uptown, I stop at the

cleaners to pick up a sweater. The clerk is in the mood to chat. He tells me he is an avid gardener, who keeps chickens in his backyard.

"Chickens in the city? Why?"

"Lots of good reasons. For the eggs, for the manure for my garden, and for sentimental reasons."

"Sentimental?"

"I grew up with chickens and just wanted them around again."

I smile. He invites me to go check them out. "Just go and see."

His home is one block east of my usual walk home. I find his address easily and go around the back to check out the chicken house. It's well-designed and attractive—like a privileged child's play house—with windows and a two-toned paint job, with a tidy screened-in area, made with (what else?) chicken wire. The chickens are beautiful—a deep auburn color, sleek and polished. Who would guess that some of my neighbors are farming in this urban area.

It wasn't easy to make it happen, apparently. The clerk told me that, in order for the city to approve his project, he had to obtain fifty signatures of his nearest neighbors in the apartment buildings on *both* sides. He said it took him months, but he persisted. Here was one man's dream realized—in his own backyard.

If I were driving, I wouldn't take the time to

interrupt the direct trajectory back to my house. But I realize that when I'm walking, everything seems to be more or less "on the way." It's easy to do an errand here, a bit of browsing there, and even to tack on a pleasant detour. Somehow going slower opens up the possibility of the unexpected.

I'm heading home mid-afternoon on a weekday after finishing a stress test at the Abbott Heart Institute in south Minneapolis. It's near the Midtown Global Market, where I've just treated myself to a spicy shrimp taco at the Sonora Grill. And I bought a bright green cotton scarf from the African vendors, because it made me feel hopeful, like spring.

I stand at the Lake Street and Chicago Avenue terminal, waiting for the westbound #21 bus. The ethnic mix of people waiting with me is as great as you'll find anywhere in Minneapolis: Afro-Americans, Hispanics, Somalians, Hmongs and whites. They are young, middle-aged and old, able bodied and no longer able bodied.

The bus fills up fast. I take a seat near the back door, next to a slightly-built middle-aged man. His black hair is turning grey at the sides, his eyes are dark and slightly slanted. His brown face suggests a mix of hispanic and black, and maybe something else. His face also suggests a hard, thin life.

After a few minutes he says. "You have a great haircut."

(This could be a line, pure and simple. And I could shut down the conversation with a cool "Thanks." But I smile, deciding to be curious, instead of wary.)

I say "Thanks" and add: "I got it at Great Clips in Uptown."

He chats some more. I offer something personal. "I just got out of the hospital. A heart stress test."

"I had one of those."

"Did you pass?"

"Yes, but I have to have another one. There's lots of stress in my life…(long pause)…kids, especially."

I wait before responding. He doesn't elaborate, but he doesn't have to.

I say: "It's all connected, isn't it. Our life and our bodies."

He says: "It's true. We're all one body."

(Now I'm really curious. Is he some kind of mystic?) I say: "True."

He says: "But there's a difference between you and me."

(What bit of wisdom, what kernel of truth will come next…?)

"You're beautiful and I'm not."

(Oh. But, I'm not annoyed. He's not pursuing. He's just being funny.)

I laugh.

He says: "I'm Larry. What's your name?"

(Exchanging names with men on a bus? I don't do that.)

I say: "Patricia."

We shake hands. The bus goes under Highway 35 near Nicollet Avenue, nearing a KMart and some high-rise low-rent apartments.

Larry says: "This is my stop."

(I'm relieved actually, that our conversation will end here. But I also want to wish him well.) I say: "Take care of your heart, Larry."

Larry stands up. Looking directly at me with a wry smile and tapping his chest, he says: "And the beat goes on."

We both smile.

On a Sunday afternoon, I take a #6 bus downtown to see the Guthrie's production of Tony Kushner's *Tiny Kushner*. I want to try a different route to cut off some walking time. Unfortunately, I get the wrong instructions from my bus driver for the connecting bus. And, running late, I miss the connection. So I hail a cab that is circulating the downtown area. I get to the theater five minutes before curtain. (My just-in-the-nick-of-time cab ride cost $6.) I buy a rush ticket—one of the last available seats—and take my place in the first row, front and center.

Afterward, I walk back along the Mississippi River, where there are beautiful new luxury townhouses and condos. I take my time, enjoying the mini gardens on private balconies.

As soon as I reach Hennepin Avenue, a #6 comes along. Sometimes, connections are amazingly easy.

Ten minutes later, on an impulse, I hop off at the bus stop at Hennepin Avenue and 27th Street. The day has turned cool and drizzly and I'm in the mood for my favorite comfort food. I walk into Roat Osha, my favorite Thai restaurant, and order shrimp pad thai to take out.

My order is ready in no time at all—I must be slightly ahead of the rush—and when I get out to the corner again, another #6 bus is just pulling up to the curb. It's all on the same fare.

My food is still toasty by the time I walk in my door. How good can it get?

Four Years Later

When I first started my carless project in January of 2009, I thought of it as an experiment. Could I do it? Would I like it? I allowed for the possibility that I might hate it. I put my car in storage for two months, knowing that I could get it back, just in case I found out that, for a 60-something woman living in Minneapolis, going carless was just not feasible.

But, after 60 days of trying it out, I found that there was much to recommend the carless life—and many unforeseen benefits. I sold my car to the man who had stored it for me.

This meant a complete shift in how I worked out my daily routines. It also meant a complete shift in mindset. I counted everything now in blocks, not miles. The mind map of my city changed dramatically. For the first time, "easy to get to" equaled "on a main bus line."

You might think that living without a car would close off options and make my world smaller, but instead my world opened up in some surprising ways. I began to see my city with new eyes and feel each day with my whole body. I experienced the sights, the sounds, and the scents in a way that I would have missed driving in my car. Walking often gave me a pleasant break in the day, which slowed me down "to the pace of guidance," as Christina Baldwin says, or helped me make the mood shift I really needed. I began to feel a solidarity with other bus riders and deep gratitude for bus drivers and for friends who offered me rides. Going carless enlarged my world and my heart.

At the same time, I learned the power of limitations and the reward of restraint. I needed to buy literally only what I could carry. It was fascinating to see how that limitation required me to buy more selectively—and significantly reduced my spending.

I needed to reserve time and energy in my day for routine errands. Limiting what I could do in a day helped me to discover my real priorities, and helped me to practice letting go of the things I really didn't need or want to do. This process gave me more unscheduled time, something I now see as a luxury and a gift.

I will not be one of those women in her 80s dreading the day her kids take away her car keys. I already know how to live well without a car. And that feels liberating.

I *am* dependent on the mass transit system in my city, on my own two feet, and occasionally on friends who drive, which makes me newly appreciative of them all. But I call that *inter*dependence and *inter*connection. And I call that good.

My carless life is simpler and in some ways far more satisfying. I feel freer, lighter, less encumbered. I have fewer costs, and far less guilt about my carbon footprint.

Americans spend an average of almost $9000 a year per vehicle on car ownership—including payments, fuel, maintenance, insurance, and depreciation.[3] I spend less than $1000 a year on buses, cabs and carfares.

I thought I might sign up with HourCar or ZipCar, but I found that my needs did not mesh with their programs. In the last four years, I have rented cars from Enterprise, but only on two occasions—one for a wedding weekend and one for an out-of-town speaking engagement.

I feel healthier, because walking is now built into my day, every day. And, in fact, I *am* healthier. Even though I am out in the elements year round, my winter colds are few and far between. I have increased my muscle strength and stamina. And even more remarkably, my bones have gotten stronger. Bone density tests before and two years after going carless showed that I've moved out of the "osteoporosis" category in my spine and my hip—and into the "osteopenia" (pre-osteoporosis) category. I improved my bone density scores significantly—not with drugs or diet—but through increased exercise alone. We've seen all the studies about the benefits of a less sedentary life. I've felt the benefits in my own body.

In all, my experiment with carless living has been a success. I've had my challenges, but, it's been almost four years now and so far, so good.

In those four years, I've made major and minor

adjustments that have made the carless life easier. I changed my dentist, my clinic, my hairstylist, and yes, my massage therapist, choosing ones closer to my part of town and easier to get to by bus. On a day-to-day basis, I'm living more locally—spending significantly less than before—and enjoying it more. And, with the money saved, I'm taking more trips, including one to Ghana, west Africa, where my California son and his family have moved.

My *carless* life has truly become my *carfree* life.

On a glorious spring morning, after an inspiring lecture in downtown Minneapolis and a pleasant stroll through the Thursday Farmer's Market on Nicollet Mall, I find a comfortable chair in the downtown library. There is an art book within easy reach on the life and work of the great Mexican painter Rufino Tamayo. I pick it up and idly browse through it, falling under the spell of his magical images. I dip into the text. Tamayo describes painting as "working with a poetical feeling within the precious limitation of the picture."

He could be describing my carfree life. "Within the precious limitation" of no longer having a car, I feel a new expansiveness. An unexpected freedom. And yes, a "poetical feeling" toward each day. Like an artist working within the limits of her canvas, I am happily composing each day as freely and as creatively as I am able.

The completely carfree life is not for everyone, to be sure. For most people in most American cities, there are too many factors working against it. It may not be for you. And it may not be for me, indefinitely.

But if you are leaning toward to the carfree life, I say, "Go for it." Try losing your wheels for a while—and see what happens. I invite you to discover for yourself the deep satisfaction—and the sheer enjoyment!—of living in the not-so-fast lane.

A Road Map to Carfree Living
81 Tips

Creating a carfree life is more than changing a habit. It's a web of large and small routines, expectations, and attitudes that start to shift over time, day by day. Here is a road map for making that shift.

Stage One. Getting Ready.

- **Vacation where you don't need a car.** See how it feels. Try Manhattan, San Francisco, Boston, Washington D.C., Portland, OR. Try Europe, Mexico, almost anywhere else in the world.

- **Keep a car diary.** Note your current car habits. Count your car trips per day, per week.

- **Make a game of it.** How much can you reduce your trips per day? Per week? Give yourself credit for improvement.

- **Resist the urge to jump in the car for a single errand.** Wait until you have at least two reasons to grab your car keys.

- **Crunch the numbers/Imagine.** Ask yourself, What would I do with money I currently spend on car repair bills? Picture your favorite luxury. Or, imagine paying off your VISA account, or making a 13th mortgage payment every year.

$1750 equals 1000 bus rides in my town.
$1000 equals 100 cab rides.
$500 equals any number of Christmas gifts, concert tickets, shoes.

- **Think outside the box.** Picture when a short bus ride would make sense. Think of a routine weekly trip that is easy to take on a bus. Mine was a Thursday morning meditation group.

- **Try it out.** Take a ride on your city bus.

- **Make the most of a single fare.** In our city, one fare is good for 2 1/2 hours, any number of rides, in any direction. That's a lot to play with.

- **Take it easy at first.** Try short rides with no connections. Then try longer, more complicated rides with one or more connections.

- **Discover what a transfer can do.** How far can you go? Can you switch from bus to light rail? And then switch back to bus? Can you get downtown and home again on one fare?

- **Collect bus schedules.** Grab a schedule for each new route you try. Every bus has its own route's schedule. The central library has them all.

- **Check out the reduced fare policies.** Note the reduced fare for persons with disabilities, students, veterans and seniors. They can be substantial. When I turned 65, my non-peak fare went from $1.75 to 75 cents.

- **Be a rider, not a driver.** Your city's sights, smells, and sounds have been there all along. You just haven't noticed because you were at the wheel. Take them in—like a tourist.

- **Explore what you can do on foot.** It's more than you think. Take in your city at a walker's pace. Feel your feet connecting to the ground. Smell the roses in your neighbor's garden.

- **Consciously slow down.** Relax. Breathe.

- **Learn the art of waiting.** Calm down. Don't worry. The bus will come, without your mental assistance or insistence.

- **Trust.** Trust the system. Trust the universe. Your bus will appear—on schedule—99% of the time. You will get where you need to go.

- **Walk, don't run.** Never run to catch a bus. It's not worth the risk. Accidents happen when you rush.

- **Look both ways.** Be vigilant crossing streets. You are a small, soft-bodied human. Cars, trucks, buses, trains and even cyclists will run you down if you are in the wrong place at the wrong time.

Stage Two. Trying It Out.

- **Allow for an awkward stage at the beginning.** This as an experiment, not a pass/fail course. Try it out for a limited period of time.

- **Stow your car keys in the junk drawer.** Make them harder to get at.

- **Play with your daily transportation options like a sudoku puzzle.** There's more than one way to get from point A to point B.

- **Let the computer plan your trips.** Check out the website for your metro transit system. Use its "trip planning" feature.

- **Miniaturize.** Reduce the size of the things you carry. You'll have to be your own trunk, backseat and glove compartment. My portable office is now in one small zip bag: cell phone, notebook, pen, business cards, post-its.

- **Create a launching pad.** Set up a place near your door for everything you need for the road: umbrella, scarf, hat, gloves, bus schedules, water bottle, etc.

- **Work with the weather.** Try mini bus rides (3 and 4 blocks) on extra cold or extra hot days. Know your walking limits. Don't over-extend. It won't be any fun.

- **Dress for comfort and health.** Wear sensible shoes. Use sunscreen.

- **Plan ahead.** Combine errands, appointments, socializing, and shopping in one trip when you can.

- **Think before you buy.** Do you really need it? Do you really love it? Save time, money and aggravation by getting it right the first time. Returning stuff on a bus is a pain.

- **Buy only what you can carry.** That's how much you can take home on a bus.

- **Invest in totes.** You'll need different sizes on different days. Also, the plastic insulated thermal bags are handy for carrying home frozen foods.

- **"I have everything I need."** Make this your new mantra, because it's usually true. I once learned to make mayonnaise from scratch, because it was easier than going back to the store for it. I already had all the ingredients. It was delicious.

- **Set new priorities.** Begin to distinguish needs from wants, necessary trips from discretionary ones, essential purchases from nonessential ones. Let "Must do today." become "It can wait."

- **Create white space in your day.** Subtract one thing from your to-do list. Drop one thing from your events calendar. When you allow more time between errands and engagements, you reduce your stress dramatically.

- **Enjoy a new flow to your day.** Your day will be in a smaller circle geographically, but it will be more alive, more vivid. You'll be feeling more a part of your neighborhood, shopping locally and enjoying it more.

- **People watch.** Watch the best reality show in town—other people on the bus. Let them into your day. It's street theater. The overheard conversations, the mini-dramas between riders and drivers. The kind gesture. The good humor. The occasional dust-up.

- **Play your role.** Realize you are seeing and being seen. It's OK to be part of the scene. In fact, it's fun. Greet your drivers. Thank them. Talk to the person next to you, if you feel like it.

Stage Three. Getting Serious.

- **Evaluate.** How is it going? What have you learned? How do you feel about it? What has changed? Any surprises? Any insights? Ready for more?

- **Give yourself credit for trying.** This isn't for everyone. And if it is for you now, it may not be forever. Things can change—the weather, your health, your work or family life.

- **If you're ready, store your car** where you can't get at it.

- **Explore the alternatives to car ownership.** Do the research for renting a car by the day— or the hour (with Zip Car or Hour Car). What are the costs, schedules, deals? What are the advantages and the disadvantages of each? Try out a few.

- **Expand your bus-riding world.** Discover the parts of your city you've ignored in the past. Go where you've never gone before.

- **Order an electronic transit card.** It's really convenient and you save more money.

- **Pick one shopping area.** Find one you like and make it yours. If you can find the basics— groceries, banking, cleaners, hardware, gifts—in one, stick with it. You'll save time, money, and aggravation. It's sanity-inducing.

- **Shop often, shop quick.** Shop on your way home. It's often easier to hop off a bus, shop, and hop on again than it is to find a parking space, shop, and get out of the lot.

- **Note your progress.** Is it easier to carry two full grocery bags now? You're getting stronger. Your muscles and your bones! After two years, my bone density test proved that.

- **Protect your feet.** Your feet will love good shoes, massage, not too much walking. Be nice to them. They are your wheels now.

- **Look for the creative solution.** Keep coloring outside the lines. If it's hard to get home by bus from the theater at night, try matinees.

- **Honor your personal preferences.** I like weekday, daytime busing best. I don't want to stand alone in the dark waiting for a bus.

- **Call a cab.** It's an affordable luxury.

- **Invest in your bike.** Get two panniers designed to carry groceries, lights, and a good lock.

- **Ride share.** Ask a friend to drive and pay your own way, so you can ask again. I offer friends $5 one way, $10 round trip. Team up with a

chorus member who can drive to rehearsals or a
colleague who is going to a week-end workshop.

- **Get creative about paying.** Some friends will
  resist taking cash. Instead, pay for their parking,
  lunch, or movie ticket.

- **Offer exchanges for your rides.** Babysit a
  friend's child. Garden. Cook a meal. What
  service do you have to offer? Take the risk and
  ask.

- **Call well in advance for rides.** Don't call
  friends with your emergencies. Always have a
  back-up strategy.

- **Be on time.** Never keep a ride-share friend
  waiting for you. Be ready to walk out the door
  when they arrive.

- **Learn the grace** of going on your friends'
  schedules, not yours.

- **Learn the grace** of going on your friends'
  preferred routes, not yours. We don't realize the
  driving ruts we are in until someone else is at
  the wheel. And now someone else is always at
  the wheel.

- **Discover what you can do without a car.**
  You can join door-knocking campaigns and alley
  clean-up projects in your neighborhood. For
  exercise, you can walk with a neighbor, instead
  of driving to a gym.

Stage Four. Carfree Living.

- **When you're ready, lose your wheels.** I sold my car after two months. It took 60 days of experimenting—in the winter—to imagine that I could do it year round.

- **You have a new part-time job.** Like any new job, carfree living comes with a learning curve, regular daily time commitments, new colleagues, increasing ease and familiarity, and progress in new skills. It's a small job with a big pay-off.

- **After you've sold your car,** allow yourself a nostalgic look back—and a reality check. Acknowledge what you loved about your car— and what's really challenging about your new lifestyle. Still OK? Alright then, keep on keeping on.

- **Claim your slower pace.** You are not in the fast lane any more. You're slowing down "to the pace of guidance." (Christina Baldwin)

- **Discover what is "enough" for you.** Notice when you can happily pass on some things to buy—or to do. Savor the feeling of sufficiency.

- **Savor the perfect at-home day.** Relish the day with no interruptions and something significant accomplished.

- **Got cabin fever?** Find a friendly coffee shop, one you can walk to, if possible. Allow yourself some regular time-out places that are easy to get to.

- **Invite friends to your place.** Now potluck dinners, book clubs, and brunches are easier to host than to get to. Consider making your home your favorite social venue.

- **Enjoy serendipitous connections.** When you are walking, you often meet your neighbors on the street, simply by chance. You stop and chat briefly. No appointment needed. It's so easy!

- **Stay open to surprises.** I found if I took a bus to a class or meeting, I could often get a ride home with someone I met there. I found I liked being outside more, befriending the weather, summer and winter. I found that if you live within the city limits in Minneapolis, our metro transit system is, as they say in the Midwest, "pretty darn good." All surprises.

- **Join the crowd.** Feel a new solidarity with young professionals on their way to work. It's hip to ride the bus because it's easy, cheap, and green. And if you want, you can text all the way. Feel a new solidarity with other riders—students, the elderly, the poor, the disabled. They gave me courage to persevere: If they can do it, maybe so can I.

- **Accept your foibles.** Propriety and vanity are mine. I won't carry toilet paper home in huge 12-roll packs, even if they are cheaper. I buy smaller packages that fit discreetly inside shopping bags. And I refuse to use a "little old lady" metal shopping cart. So far, anyway.

- **Don't let routine bus rides get routine.** Try a new route home sometimes. Transfer on and off the light rail to shorten a multi-bus crosstown ride. Allow time for a new discovery.

- **Discover "Everything is on the way."** For riders and walkers, small detours and quicks stops—popping into a new shop, for example—are easy and fun.

- **Get out of town.** When you're ready, make wider circles. Go to another city by Greyhound or another intercity line. You may find this surprisingly doable.

- **Don't give up.** When it's just too hard to bus to a particular destination, or too expensive to go by cab, change the destination. For example, if the ride to your dentist is difficult, which it was for me, find a new one closer to you.

- **Cultivate contentment.** One summer day I realized—for that day—I was perfectly content to move in circles no larger than my feet or my bike could take me.

Stage Five. Savor the Rewards.

- **Measure your FINANCIAL BENEFITS of the carfree life.** By not owning a car, your savings are bigger than you think. Americans spend an average of $9000 a year per vehicle.[4]

- **Don't Worry. Be Happy.** You don't have to worry about rising gas prices, repair bills, parking fees and fine, tags, insurance, or replacement costs. You are carfree and carefree.

- **Measure the ENVIRONMENTAL BENEFITS.** These too are amazing. Driving your car is by far the biggest part of your carbon footprint. Everything else pales in comparison.

- **Measure the UNFORESEEN BENEFITS.**

  PHYSICAL. Healthier. More sunshine and fresh air. Less sedentary, stronger.

  EMOTIONAL. Less stress, better mood, a slower pace of life. Feeling connected to your city, more and deeper connection with friends. In a word, happier.

  MENTAL. More expansive, adventurous. More confident, self-reliant. More optimistic, positive. Relief from financial pressure and responsibilities of car ownership.

SPIRITUAL. Less judgment. Less guilt about your carbon footprint. More freedom. More patience. More trust. More compassion. More gratitude. More contentment.

- **Experience the joy of a balanced, not-so-fast life.** Walking is good for your body. Waiting grounds you and makes you quietly receptive. Riding is far less stressful than driving. Each day becomes calmer, more spacious, more focused. Relationships go wider and deeper in the not-so-fast lane. Satisfaction increases.

Savor your accomplishment.
You've made a major lifestyle shift.
That's huge. Congratulations!

Endnotes

1. AAA's 62nd annual "Your Driving Costs" study shows what Americans spend annually to own and operate a vehicle. The 2012 overall average is 59.6 cents per mile, or $8,946 per year, based on 15,000 miles of annual driving. For 4WD SUVs, average costs go up to $11,360 per vehicle per year. For large sedans, average costs are $11,324 per vehicle. For compact models, average costs are $6,735 per vehicle. Costs include monthly payment, fuel, maintenance, insurance, license and registration fees, taxes, depreciation and finance charges. Source: AAA.com, "Your Driving Costs," http://newsroom.aaa.com/wp-content/uploads/2012/04/YourDrivingCosts2012.pdf

2. Global vehicle ownership per capita in 2010 was 148 vehicles in operation per 1000 people. Vehicle ownership per capita in the U.S. is the highest in the world with 769 vehicles in operation per 1000 people. The U.S. has the largest fleet of motor vehicles in the world, with 239.8 million. The People's Republic of China has the second largest fleet in the world, with slightly more than 78 million vehicles. Source: John Sousanis, "World Vehicle Population Tops 1 Billion Units." *Ward AutoWorld*, August 15, 2011. http://wardsauto.com/ar/world_vehicle_population_110815

3. AAA, "Your Driving Costs."

4. Ibid.

Your Carfree Notes

Your Carfree Notes

Your Carfree Notes

Your Carfree Notes

Your Carfree Notes

Your Carfree Notes

Watch your step now. That last one is a big one. Have a lovely day!

—Minneapolis MetroTransit Bus Driver

17922174R00064

Made in the USA
Charleston, SC
07 March 2013